CREEPY CRAWLIES

This I-SPY book belongs to:_____

Introduction

One group of Creepy Crawlies, the insects, are the most successful animals on Earth. So far, scientists have managed to identify about one and a half million different kinds of insects. And there is no part of the globe, nor any type of habitat where insects cannot live, and there are a few kinds that live in the sea. Some scientists think that there might even be another 30 million kinds of insects yet to be identified and named!

Not all Creepy Crawlies are insects; there are spiders, wood lice, centipedes, and millipedes among others. People often mistake these creatures for insects, but all insects have six legs while spiders have eight, wood lice have ten, and centipedes many more. And then there are slugs and snails, worms and other creatures which slither, like snakes. Look around you; you'll find Creepy Crawlies in all sorts of places you might not expect!

How to use your I-SPY book

The Creepy Crawlies in this book are arranged in groups, from slugs and snails through to pond creatures and snakes. Don't forget that almost all adult insects have wings while the young grubs or caterpillars do not. So even though we've shown the adult butterflies and moths in most cases, for example, if you know what their grubs look like and you Spy one, you can score for that instead.

You need 1000 points to send off for your I-Spy certificate (see page 64) but that is not too difficult because there are masses of points in every book. As you make each I-Spy, write your score in the box and, where there is a question, double your score if you can answer it. Check your answer against the correct one on page 63.

BRANDLING WORM

Scientific name Eisenia foetida

Not all earthworms live in the soil. You will have to look for the brandling worm in the compost heap at the bottom of the garden.

What do earthworms feed on?

 I - SPY points: 5, double with answer

GARDEN SNAIL

Scientific name Helix aspersa

You are most likely to find snails on the move after it has rained, or if you go out into the garden as it is getting dark. They tend to stay hidden in hot weather however.

I - SPY points: 5

BANDED SNAIL

Scientific name Cepaea species

There are a number of different species of banded snail, yellow, brown or pink, with or without bands. Look for them in gardens, hedgerows or on sand dunes.

I - SPY **points: 15**

GREAT GREY SLUG

Scientific name Limax maximus

Like snails, slugs tend to come out after rain or in the cool of the evening, as they dry out very quickly if they stay in the sun.

I - SPY **points: 15**

GREAT BLACK SLUG

Scientific name Arion ater

This slug can be black, brown or orange. Because slugs feed on the leaves, stems and roots of plants this makes them very unpopular with farmers and gardeners.

I - SPY **points: 10**

AZURE DAMSELFLY

Scientific name
Coenagrion puella

Blue damselflies are common around ponds and lakesides during the summer. Here the green female of the pair is laying eggs in the stem of a water plant, while the blue male stands on guard.

 I - SPY points: 10, double with laying eggs

LARGE RED DAMSELFLY

Scientific name
Pyrrhosoma nymphula

The earliest of the damselflies appear from late spring onwards. This pair is mating in what is called the 'wheel position'.

 I - SPY points: 10, double for the wheel position

BEAUTIFUL DEMOISELLE DAMSELFLY

Scientific name
Calopteryx virgo

Look out for the demoiselle damselflies, there are two types of species that live beside ponds, lakes, canals, rivers and streams. They will, however, hunt away from water and may end up in your back garden.

 I - SPY points: 15

COMMON DARTER DRAGONFLY

Scientific name
Sympetrum striolatum

While damselflies hold their wings over the body at rest, dragonflies hold them out to the side. The common darter male is red but the female is yellowish with dark markings.

I - SPY points: 10

BROAD-BODIED CHASER DRAGONFLY

Scientific name
Libellula depressa

This lovely dragonfly is in the habit of visiting and even breeding in garden ponds. While the male is blue the female is golden in colour.

 I - SPY points: 15

GOLDEN-RINGED DRAGONFLY

Scientific name
Cordulegaster boltonii

This is one of the large darter dragonflies, which lives near moving water. You may also score points if you see one of the other darter dragonflies with blue or green body markings.

I - SPY points: 20

LACEWING

Scientific name Nineta flava

Lacewings get their name from the network of veins in their wings. Although they look delicate, they have strong jaws and feed on aphids and other tiny insects.

○ **I - SPY** points: 15

ALDERFLY

Scientific name Sialis lutaria

Alderflies are found in large numbers in early summer on waterside plants where the females lay large batches of eggs. Like those of Lacewings, their wings have a network of veins.

○ **I - SPY** points: 20

CADDISFLY

Scientific name

Philopotamus montanus

Caddisflies look rather like moths but they have hairs on their wings instead of scales. They feed on nectar and most kinds are active at night.

◯ **I - SPY** points: **15**

COMMON SCORPION-FLY

Scientific name

Panorpa communis

These insects are quite harmless despite their name, which is derived from the appearance of the male shown here. They actually eat plant sap and dead insects.

◯ **I - SPY** points: **15**

GREEN DRAKE MAYFLY

Scientific name
Ephemera danica

Most kinds of mayflies appear as adults (the winged insects) in May. They usually live long enough to find a mate – up to about four days only.

I - SPY points: 25

SMALL YELLOW SALLY STONEFLY

Scientific name
Chloroperla torrentium

Adult Stoneflies are usually found close to running water and, although they can fly, they often spend much of their time hiding among plants.

I - SPY points: 25

SILVERFISH

Scientific name
Lepisma saccharina

◯   I - SPY points: 15

Silverfish belong to an ancient group of insects called bristletails. Silverfish often live in nooks and crannies in kitchens where they come out at night to feed on food scraps.

COMMON EARWIG

Scientific name
Forficula auricularia

Earwigs get their name from the mistaken idea that they will crawl into people's ears. They do usually hide in small crevices and do not often fly, even though they can!

◯   I - SPY points: 5

11

SPECKLED BUSH-CRICKET

Scientific name

Leptophyes punctatissima

Bush Crickets look like Grasshoppers with long feelers but they do not jump as freely, preferring to walk around the plants on which they feed.

 **I - SPY** points: 15

MEADOW GRASSHOPPER

Scientific name

Chorthippus parallelus

Grasshoppers are usually found in grassland. They 'sing' by rubbing their legs against a hard vein on their front wings.

 **I - SPY** points: 5

Great Washbourne

12

FOREST BUG

Scientific name Pentatoma rufipes

Shield Bugs are shield shaped but they are also known as 'Stink Bugs' because of the very strong and unpleasant smell, which they produce in order to deter predators.

○ **I - SPY** points: 20

DOCK BUG

Scientific name Coreus marginatus

As its name implies this bug is commonly found on docks and sorrels, on seeds of which the young bugs feed. It may be seen across much of southern Britain as far up as the south midlands.

○ **I - SPY** points: 20

POTATO CAPSID BUG

Scientific name
Calocoris norvegicus

There are many species of capsid bug, most with the general shape of this species. The potato capsid is often found in gardens where it likes to sit at the centre of cultivated members of the daisy family.

○ **I - SPY** points: 10

13

ALDER SPITTLEBUG, A FROGHOPPER

Scientific name Aphrophora alni

The froghopper is a kind of bug so-named because it tends to sit froglike with the head raised. This species is found on a wide variety of plants and can be common in gardens.

I - SPY points: 10

SPITTLE BUGS

Scientific name Family Cercopidae

These are young froghoppers, also called cuckoo-spit insects, because they stop themselves from drying up and hide by surrounding their bodies with a kind of froth.

Why should the froth be called 'Cuckoo-spit'?

I - SPY points: 10, double with answer

BLACK-AND-RED FROGHOPPER

I - SPY points: 20

Scientific name
Cercopis vulnerata

A strikingly marked species of froghopper, the black and red colours indicating that is is probably distasteful and predators should avoid it. Numbers vary considerably from year to year.

PEA APHIDS

Scientific name
Acyrthosiphon pisum

Aphids are tiny plant bugs, which feed on a wide variety of plants and many of them are pests. Score for any species that you come across during your searches.

I - SPY points: 5

15

GATEKEEPER BUTTERFLY

Scientific name
Pyronia tithonus

The Gatekeeper Butterfly is quite common. It is also known as the Hedge Brown, which suggests where it is most often to be seen.

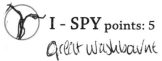 I - SPY points: 5

Great Washbourne

MEADOW BROWN BUTTERFLY

Scientific name Maniola jurtina

This is a common butterfly of rough grassland, appearing in early summer. Like all of the British brown butterflies, its caterpillars feed on various grasses.

I - SPY points: 5

RINGLET BUTTERFLY

Scientific name
Aphantopus hyperantus

The ringlet is a dark brown butterfly and it gets its name from the black and white circles on the undersides of its wings.

○ **I - SPY** points: 15

SPECKLED WOOD BUTTERFLY

Scientific name
Pararge aegeria tircis

The brown and yellow markings on the wings of this butterfly make it hard to see as it flits among the trees.

○ **I - SPY** points: 5

MARBLED WHITE BUTTERFLY

Scientific name
Melanargia galathea

Despite its name, the marbled white is in the same family as the brown butterflies and is not related to the cabbage whites. It is found in rough pasture during mid-summer.

 **I - SPY** points: 15

SMALL PEARL-BORDERED FRITILLARY BUTTERFLY

Scientific name Boloria selene

These butterflies get their name because of the pattern of spots on an orangey back ground. Some kinds live mainly in woods while others are found in open country.

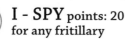 **I - SPY** points: 20
for any fritillary

SMALL TORTOISESHELL BUTTERFLY

Scientific name Aglais urticae

The small tortoise shell is often abundant in some years. It appears in early summer and is often seen on the 'Butterfly Bush', the buddleia. Its caterpillars feed on nettles.

I - SPY points: 5

Great Washbourne

RED ADMIRAL BUTTERFLY

Scientific name
Vanessa atalanta

This large, brightly coloured butterfly is usually first seen in May or June but, although it is a Mediterranean insect, some individuals do manage to survive the harsh British winter.

I - SPY points: 10

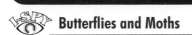

PAINTED LADY BUTTERFLY

Scientific name Vanessa cardui

This is another Mediterranean butterfly which travels to Britain in May and June, often in huge numbers. This brightly coloured butterfly lays its eggs on thistles and nettles.

 I - SPY points: 15

COMMA BUTTERFLY

Scientific name Polygonia c-album

The comma has tattered looking wings for camouflage but it is the pale comma-shaped markings on the underwings which give this butterfly its name.

I - SPY points: 15

PEACOCK BUTTERFLY

Scientific name Inachis io

This large, brightly coloured insect may be seen during April and May and then again in September and October.

How does it get its name?

I - SPY points: 10, double with answer

LARGE SKIPPER BUTTERFLY

Scientific name
Ochlodes venatus

Skippers look more like moths than butterflies. They get their name because they beat their wings quickly and 'skip' from place to place so they are hard to spot.

I - SPY points: 15

COMMON BLUE BUTTERFLY

Scientific name
Polyommatus icarus

Blue butterflies are usually found on grassland, commons, heaths and downs. The female common blue is a brownish colour.

I - SPY points: 20

Great Washoune

ORANGE TIP BUTTERFLY

Scientific name
Anthocharis cardamines

The orange-tip is a member of the white butterfly family and it is easy to see how it gets its name. Note that the female does not have orange tips to the forewings.

I - SPY points: 5

LARGE WHITE BUTTERFLY

Scientific name Pieris brassicae

The large white is the largest of the three common species of white butterflies found in the British Isles. Not as big is the similar-looking small white and the green-veined white, which has noticeable lines on the underwings.

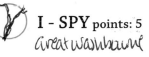

I - SPY points: 5

great washbourne

LARGE WHITE BUTTERFLY CATERPILLARS

Scientific name Pieris brassicae

The caterpillars of large whites will feed on plants of the cabbage family, which is why they are sometimes called cabbage whites and why they are unpopular with gardeners.

I - SPY points: 10

CLOUDED YELLOW BUTTERFLY

Scientific name Colias croceus

In Britain, this is usually a rare butterfly but, from time to time, large numbers may migrate to Britain from continental Europe.

I - SPY points: 20

BRIMSTONE BUTTERFLY

Scientific name
Gonepteryx rhamni

While the male is pale yellow, the female brimstone is greenish-white. Adults may even be seen flying during the winter months on suitable warm days.

I - SPY points: 10

6-SPOT BURNET MOTH

Scientific name
Zygaena filipendulae

The burnets are day-fliers when they can often be found visiting flowers to feed. Their bright colours warn possible predators that they are not good to eat. The caterpillars take in the poison from the plants on which they feed.

I - SPY points: 10

PEPPERED MOTH CATERPILLAR

Scientific name Biston betularia

The long, stick-like caterpillars of the peppered moth have three pairs of legs at the front of the body and four 'claspers' at the back with no legs between. They move by 'looping'.

I - SPY points: 15

PRIVET HAWK MOTH

Scientific name Sphinx ligustri

Wherever privet hedges grow so you are likely to find this large moth. When disturbed it opens its wings to reveal the pink markings, a warning to predators.

I - SPY points: 20

LARGE ELEPHANT HAWK MOTH

Scientific name Deilephila elpenor

This very beautiful moth is fairly common and may be found from May onwards, quite often in gardens. The small elephant hawk is similar but with less pink on the wings.

 I - SPY points: 15, for either elephant hawk moth

LARGE ELEPHANT HAWK MOTH CATERPILLAR

Scientific name Deilephila elpenor

This very striking caterpillar, which may be mistaken for a small snake, reaches 90mm (3½in) in length and feeds on willowherb.

I - SPY points: 10

HUMMING-BIRD HAWK MOTH

Scientific name
Macroglossum stellatarum

The adult moth hovers in front of a flower and uses its long coiled tongue to collect nectar. Some people actually think they have seen a humming bird when they spot this visitor from Europe.

I - SPY points: 20

EYED HAWK MOTH

Scientific name
Smerinthus ocellata

When at rest, this moth sits with its wings closed but when disturbed it opens the forewings sideways to reveal the hindwings, each of which has a large eye-mark on it.

I - SPY points: 20

EYED HAWK MOTH CATERPILLAR

Scientific name
Smerinthus ocellata : Sphingidae

The main food plants of this caterpillar are willows, sallows and apple, so look for it on the apple trees in your garden or orchard. Like many hawk moth caterpillars, it has a horn on the tail.

I - SPY points: 15

BUFF-TIP MOTH

Scientific name
Phalera bucephala

Buff-tip Moths look a bit like a broken stick when they are at rest. Because of their dull colours, they are sometimes called smudge moths.

I - SPY points: 20

BUFF-TIP MOTH CATERPILLAR

Scientific name
Phalera bucephala

These hairy caterpillars stay together in a group when small, splitting up as they get bigger. Look for them on oak, elm, lime and hazel trees.

I - SPY points: 10

GARDEN TIGER MOTH

Scientific name Arctia caja

Tiger moths taste unpleasant and the bright colours of the moth's hind wings warn birds to leave them alone. The pattern of the forewings probably helps to break up the insect's outline.

I - SPY points: 20

GARDEN TIGER MOTH CATERPILLAR

Scientific name Arctia caja

You are actually much more likely to come across a 'woolly bear', (the nickname for a tiger moth caterpillar), than find the adult moth. They feed on a wide variety of plants and are often found in gardens.

I - SPY points: 10

CINNABAR MOTH

Scientific name
Tyria (Callimorpha) jacobaea

The brightly coloured cinnabar moth is again warning birds that it is poisonous and they should not try to eat it. These moths fly by day and night.

◯ I - SPY points: 15

CINNABAR MOTH CATERPILLAR

Scientific name
Tyria (Callimorpha) jacobaea

There is no mistaking the black-and-yellow striped caterpillars of the cinnabar moth. One of their favourite foods is ragwort and they are quite useful to us by destroying this plant, which is dangerous to horses.

◯ I - SPY points: 5

BURNISHED BRASS MOTH

Scientific name
Diachrisia (= Plusia) chrysitis

These moths are part of a very large family, which all tend to have rather dull coloured front wings. With its shiny, metallic patches this is one of the exceptions.

◯ I - SPY points: 20

ANGLE SHADES MOTH

Scientific name
Phlogophora meticulosa

When at rest on a dead, brown leaf, the dull colours and patterning on the forewings of this moth make it very hard for an enemy to see.

◯ I - SPY points: 20

MARSH BROWN-EDGED TIPULA CRANE FLY

Scientific name Tipula oleraceae

Crane flies are sometimes called 'daddy-long-legs' and the weak-flying adults usually appear from summer to autumn.

What name is given to the larva of the crane fly?

I - SPY points: 5, double with answer

HOUSE GNAT

Scientific name Culex pipiens

Small mosquitoes are often called gnats. It is the female which feeds on blood, usually that of birds. The males have hairy feelers, which they use to 'hear' the wingbeats of the females.

I - SPY points: 15

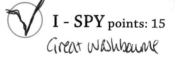

NOTCH-HORNED CLEG

Scientific name
Haematopota pluvialis

Female horse flies, or clegs, drink blood by biting animals including domestic cattle, but also bite humans. A horse fly bite can be painful and will cause the area to swell. Not pleasant!

✓ I - SPY points: 15
Great Washbourne

BLACK-RIMMED SNOUT HOVER FLY

Scientific name
Rhingia campestris

This unmistakeable fly, with its bulbous 'nose', is common in spring and early summer, when it may be found feeding from a wide range of flowers. It is especially fond of apple blossom.

I - SPY points: 10

WASP-MIMIC HOVER FLY

Scientific name
Sphaerophoria scripta

These wasp-like insects get their
name for their ability to hover
in the air. They cannot sting,
however, but their appearance
fools their enemies into thinking
that they are dangerous.

○ **I - SPY** points: 5

SHINING-FACED DRONE FLY

Scientific name Eristalis tenax

The drone fly is quite a good
mimic of the hive bee. Like the
hive bee it feeds on pollen and
the two may often be found
together on the same flower.

○ **I - SPY** points: 10

BUMBLE BEE PLUME-HORN, A HOVER FLY

I - SPY points: 15

Scientific name
Volucella bombylans

This hover fly has forms mimicking both white-tailed and red-tailed bumble bees. It lays its eggs in bumble bee nests, where the larvae feed on bits and pieces discarded by the bees.

HOVER FLY LARVA

Scientific name Syrphus ribesii

Wherever you find a plant with aphids on it so you are likely to find the larvae of hover flies. They are quite important in helping to control aphid numbers, getting through several at a single meal.

I - SPY points: 15

BLUEBOTTLE FLY

Scientific name Calliphora vicina

Male bluebottles feed on nectar but the female often buzzes loudly into the house in search of meat on which to lay its eggs. These flies may spend the winter hiding in houses.

I - SPY points: 5

GREENBOTTLE FLY

Scientific name Lucilia caesar

Like bluebottles, greenbottles are 'blow flies', for when they lay their eggs on meat, the maggots feed on the meat – it is then said to be 'blown'.

 Cw eat wasworm

I - SPY points: 5

MICHELIN

COMMON HOUSE FLY

Scientific name Musca domestica

This fly is always an unwanted visitor to our homes, since it can spread germs of one kind or another. It can be confused with the lesser house fly which is smaller and is the one which flies in circles around ceiling lights.

I - SPY points: 5

Great Wasuhbourne

COMMON YELLOW DUNG FLY

Scientific name
Scathophaga stercoraria

As its name suggests, the female of this bright-yellow furry-looking fly lays its eggs on cattle droppings. When they hatch, the grubs feed on the dung, helping to break down the manure.

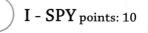

I - SPY points: 10

COMMON AWL ROBBER FLY

Scientific name
Neoitamus cyanurus

Robber flies feed by attacking other insects and sucking out the contents of their bodies. They have stiff hairs on their legs, which help them to grip on to their victims.

I - SPY points: 15

MARSH CLEAR-WINGED SNIPE FLY

Scientific name Rhagio tringarius

It is generally thought that these rather 'wasp like' flies prey on other insects, and their larvae certainly do.

I - SPY points: 20

DARK-EDGED BEE FLY

Scientific name
Bombylius major

Look out for this fly from early spring onwards, when it may be found visiting flowers such as celandine and primrose. Note how it hovers in mid air as it feeds on nectar with its long proboscis.

I - SPY points: 20

FLESH FLY

Scientific name
Sarcophaga carnaria

Called flesh flies because their maggots can feed on the flesh of open wounds. More commonly the maggots feed on dead animals. Flesh flies are seldom found in houses, unlike the similar-looking bluebottle.

I - SPY points: 10

ST MARK'S FLY

Scientific name Bibio pomonae

During spring and early summer these flies can be very numerous. They are very clumsy in flight and the males have much bigger eyes than the females.

I - **SPY** points: 5

NOONDAY FLY

Scientific name
Mesembrina meridiana

Look for the adult fly on flowers, especially brambles, in late summer and autumn. You may also find them on cow dung, on which they lay their eggs. Their maggots eat the larvae of other insects feeding on the dung.

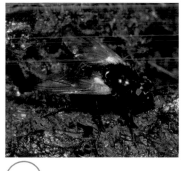

I - **SPY** points: 15

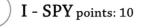

DANCE FLY

Scientific name Empis livida

Dance fly adults feed mainly on other flies, which they catch in mid air and spear on their long proboscis. Look out for mating pairs with the female hanging below the male as she feeds on the gift of a fly, which he has presented to her.

SMALL FRUIT FLY

Scientific name
Drosophila funebris

These little flies are especially attracted to rotting fruit and vegetables and can turn up in huge numbers on compost heaps. They may also be seen buzzing around the top of an open wine bottle.

I - SPY points: 15

I - SPY points: 10

BLACK ANT

Scientific name Lasius niger

Look for the black ant in your garden and do not forget that it is the female worker ants which have no wings; the Queen ant and the males have wings and can fly.

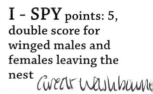

I - SPY points: 5, double score for winged males and females leaving the nest *Great Washbourne*

YELLOW MEADOW ANTS

Scientific name Lasius flavus

Meadow ants nest in a mound. They keep root aphids in their nest, which are kept in 'herds' like cows so that the ants can feed on the honeydew, which the aphids produce.

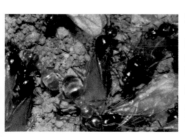

I - SPY points: 10

WOOD ANT

Scientific name Formica rufa

The huge mound of leaves, sticks and other plant material is the nest of the wood ant. It favours dry woodland for its nest and is our biggest ant.

I - SPY points: 15

GERMAN WASP

Scientific name
Vespula germanica

Wasps build nests made from a papery material, which the Queen wasp, and then the workers, make by chewing up pieces of wood. In late summer when the colony breaks up, the workers search for sweet foods.

I - SPY points: 5, Double score for one scraping wood to make paper as here

HORNET

Scientific name
Vespa crabro vexator

Although these brown and orange wasps are bigger than the more common black and yellow wasps, they are not usually aggressive and will rarely sting people.

○ **I - SPY** points: 20

RUBY-TAILED WASP

Scientific name Chrysis ignita

These little insects are not that uncommon and will be found on walls and fences searching for the nest holes of solitary wasps or other species in which to lay their eggs.

○ **I - SPY** points: 15

BUFF-TAILED BUMBLE BEE

Scientific name Bombus terrestris

Bumble bees live in smaller colonies than honey bees. Some workers suck up nectar while others collect pollen. As they pass from flower to flower, they pollinate the plants.

I - SPY points: 5

RED-TAILED BUMBLE BEE

Scientific name Bombus lapidarius

The red-tailed bumble bee, as with other bumble bees, is less common than it used to be, being more abundant in some years than others. Its red 'tail' is a giveaway in identifying it.

I - SPY points: 15

HONEY BEE

Scientific name Apis mellifera

There may be many thousands of worker bees (females that cannot breed) in one hive. The workers defend the nest and collect nectar, which they feed to the bee grubs.

What are male bees called?

 I - SPY points: 5, double with answer

LARGE GARDEN LEAF-CUTTER BEE

Scientific name Megachile willughbiella

Round or oval lumps cut out of the leaves of roses and other garden plant are usually the work of leafcutter bees. The bits of leaf are used to make chambers, which they fill with pollen to feed their developing larvae.

 I - SPY points: 15, double for finding one cutting a leaf

SANGUINE MINING BEE

Scientific name
Andrena haemorrhoa

Look out for what look like tiny volcanoes on lawns and at the side of earth paths for these are the nest entrances of mining bees. If you are lucky you will see the female peering out from the entrance, as here.

◯ **I - SPY** points: 15

WOOLCARDER BEE

Scientific name
Anthidium manicatum

The appearance of the woolcarder bee tends to coincide with the flowering of the woundworts in our gardens and hedgerows. Watch out for the larger male as he patrols a patch of these plants, often hovering in mid air.

◯ **I - SPY** points: 15

MASON BEE

Scientific name Osmia rufa

This springtime bee is so-called because it often builds its mud nest in cracks in old masonry. In large colonies they can dig out enough soft lime mortar to cause damage to the wall.

◯ **I - SPY** points: 10

DEVIL'S COACH-HORSE BEETLE

Scientific name

Ocypus (= Staphylinus) olens

You are more likely to see this beetle at night unless you disturb one from under a stone. But beware, the devil's coach horse is aggressive and can inflict a painful bite.

I - SPY points: 15

I - SPY points: 15, double with answer

COCKCHAFER

Scientific name

Melolontha melolontha

These large beetles usually emerge in May or June when they sometimes fly into lighted windows.

What other common name is given to them?

 **Beetles**

MICHELIN

SOLDIER BEETLE

Scientific name
Rhagonycha fulva

Soldier Beetles are most
commonly found on flowers,
where they feed upon small
visiting insects and also pollen.

BUMBLE-DOR BEETLE

Scientific name
Geotrupes stercorarius

Dor beetle larvae feed on dung.
The word 'dor' comes from an
Old English word which means
'buzzing insect' or even 'bumble
bee' and, when they are in
flight, dor beetles do make a
buzzing noise.

I - SPY points: 10

Great washbourne

I - SPY points: 15

7-SPOT LADYBIRD

Scientific name
Coccinella 7-punctata

Everyone knows the ladybird.
There are both red and yellow
species with different numbers of
spots. The bright colours warn
enemies that they are unpleasant
to eat.

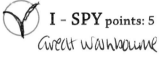 **I - SPY** points: 5

Great Washbourne

RED-HEADED CARDINAL BEETLE

Scientific name
Pyrochroa serraticornis

There are three species of cardinal
beetle in Britain, all bright red but
the less common two have black
on them. Nettle patches are often
a good place to look for them.

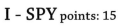 **I - SPY** points: 15

SPOTTED LONGHORN BEETLE

Scientific name
Strangalia maculata

This very common beetle is a ready flier and is best sought for around flowering brambles, for it feeds from the flowers.

Why is it called a longhorn beetle?

 I - SPY points: 15, double with answer

WASP BEETLE

Scientific name Clytus arietus

The wasp beetle is well-named for it does indeed resemble a wasp at first glance. It is usually found around trees and if you are lucky you may find a female laying her eggs into old wood.

 I - SPY points: 10

CLICK BEETLE

Scientific name
Athous haemorrhoidalis

Called a click beetle because
of the click which can be heard
when when escaping from
predators. Pick one up and not
only will you hear the click but
you will also see how effective the
system is.

 I - **SPY** points: 15

BURYING BEETLE

Scientific name
Nicrophorus vespillo

Also called a sexton beetle this
insect is associated with the
corpses of dead animals upon
which it lays its eggs and on
which its larvae feed. Not nice
to look for but interesting all
the same.

I - **SPY** points: 20

GREEN TORTOISE BEETLE

Scientific name Cassida viridis

Look for this beetle on white dead-nettle and mints. A very similar looking species can be found on creeping thistles. Both are well camouflaged and not easy to find.

I - SPY points: 15, for any tortoise beetle

THICK-LEGGED FLOWER BEETLE MALE

Scientific name
Oedemera nobilis

This beetle can be very common in early summer and is best looked for on yellow flowers such as dandelions and its relations. The female is a dull green and does not have thick legs.

I - SPY points: 10

VIOLET GROUND BEETLE

Scientific name
Carabus violaceus

The violet ground beetle is the gardener's and farmer's friend for it feeds on slugs, which is what this one is doing. The violet colour is only obvious when the beetle is looked at, from the right angle, otherwise it appears just black.

I - SPY points: 10

COMMON OIL-BEETLE

Scientific name
Meloe proscarabaeus

Also called blister beetles it is best not to handle them for they release an unpleasant liquid used to warn off anything which tries to eat them.

I - SPY points: 15

ACORN WEEVIL

Scientific name Curculio venosus

Weevils are beetles that have their biting jaws on the end of a snout, which can vary in length depending on the species. The acorn weevil is one of the long-snouted types.

I - SPY points: 10, for a long snouted weevil

 **Crustaceans**

WOODLICE

Scientific name Porcellio scaber

Woodlice are not insects; they are related to crabs and lobsters. During the day they hide in cool, dark places and come out at night to feed.

How many legs does a Woodlouse have?

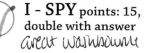 I - SPY points: 15, double with answer

Great washbourne

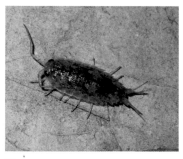

SEA SLATER

Scientific name Ligia oceanica

You will have to be beside the sea to find this relative of the woodlouse. It lives on rocks and cliffs above the high tide line.

I - SPY points: 15

WIRE-LEGGED HARVESTMAN

Scientific name
Leiobunum rotundum

Although they resemble spiders and are related to them, harvestmen are not 'true spiders'. Like spiders they are predators feeding on small insects.

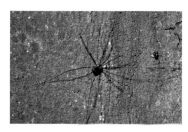

I - SPY points: 10

Great wawwawne

I - SPY points: 5

HOUSE SPIDER

Scientific name
Tegenaria gigantea

Despite its name, the house spider may also be found under logs and in holes in banks. Females are larger than males and may reach almost 2 cm (3/4 in) in body length.

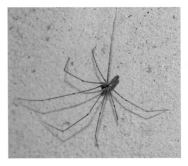

RAFTER SPIDER

Scientific name
Pholcus phalangioides

This easily recognisable spider builds its untidy web in the corner of houses, sheds and garages where the temperature is not likely to drop below 10ºC (50ºF).
It often feeds on the much larger house spider.

I - SPY points: 10

GARDEN SPIDER

Scientific name
Araneus diadematus

This spider may vary in colour from pale brown to reddish-ginger. It is found in gardens, woodlands, and heath lands. Look out for the white markings on its back, which form a cross shape.

I - SPY points: 15

COMMON FLOWER SPIDER

Scientific name Misumena vatia

This crab spider is usually found on flowers, where it lies in wait to catch its prey. It has the ability to change colour to yellow and back to white, the change taking a few hours to complete.

I - SPY points: 15

SPOTTED WOLF SPIDER

Scientific name Pardosa amentata

These spiders get their name because it was once thought that they hunted in packs. They do run along the ground very quickly but are most often found 'sunbathing' on a suitable log or stone.

I - SPY points: 5

SUNSHINE JUMPER

Scientific name
Heliophanus flavipes

Search for this jumping spider running around on plants in the garden, or for the equally common, black-and-white, zebra spider on the outside of your house. Both are best sought for on sunny days.

I - SPY points: 10

COMMON CENTIPEDE

Scientific name
Lithobius forficatus

You can sometimes find centipedes hiding under stones or logs. Despite their name, which means '100 legs', they can have as few as 34 legs or as many as 300 or more!

I - SPY points: 10

I - SPY points: 15

MILLIPEDE

Scientific name
Ommatoiulus sabulosus

The difference between these creatures and centipedes is that, for each body segment, they have two pairs of legs rather than one. As its name suggests it rolls into a ball when disturbed.

TOOTHED PONDSKATER BUG

 **I - SPY** points: 15

Scientific name
Gerris odontogaster

Pondskaters are also known as the waterstriders. The middle pair of legs is much longer than the others and is used to 'row' the insect across the surface of the water.

WATER MEASURER

Scientific name
Hydrometra stagnorum

This insect gets its name from the way it carefully walks along the surface of the water at the edge of a pond. It feeds on water fleas, mosquito larvae and small, drowned insects.

I - SPY points: 15

WHIRLIGIG BEETLE

Scientific name
Gyrinus substriatus

Whirligig beetles are found on the open areas of ponds, where groups of them scoot around the surface in an almost endless movement in search of small prey below and on the surface of the water.

I - SPY points: 15

AMBER SNAIL

Scientific name Succinea putris

Look for this snail with its rather glass-like shell on plants beside ponds, streams, rivers and canals.

I - SPY points: 10

Index

First published by Michelin Maps and Guides 2009
© Michelin, Propriétaires Éditeurs 2009.
Michelin and the Michelin Man are registered Trademarks of Michelin.
Created and produced by Blue Sky Publishing Limited. All rights reserved. No part of this publication may be reproduced, copied or transmitted in any form without the prior consent of the publisher. Print services by FingerPrint International Book production - fingerprint@pandora.be
The publisher gratefully acknowledges the contribution of the I-Spy team: Camilla Lovell and Ruth Neilson in the production of this title.
The publisher gratefully acknowledges the contribution of Premaphotos Wildlife who provided all the photographs and the text in this I-Spy book.
Reprinted 2015 15 14 13 12 11 10 9

Answers: P3 Earthworms feed on rotting vegetable matter. **P14** They first appear around the time that the cuckoo returns to Britain. **P21** The eyespots on the wings are similar to those on the tail feathers of the bird or the cuckoo name. **P33** The larva is called a leatherjacket. **P47** Male bees are called drones. **P49** They are called maybugs. **P52** Because it has very long antennae, its 'feelers'. **P56** They have 5 pairs of legs.

HOW TO GET YOUR I-SPY CERTIFICATE AND BADGE

Every time you score 1000 points or more in an I-Spy book, you can apply for a certificate

Here's what to do, step by step:

Certificate

- Ask an adult to check your score
- Ask his or her permission to apply for a certificate
- Apply online to www.ispymichelin.com
- Enter your name and address and the completed title
- We will send you back via e mail your certificate for the title

Badge

- Each I-Spy title has a cut out (page corner) token at the back of the book
- Collect five tokens from different I-Spy titles
- Put Second Class Stamps on two strong envelopes
- Write your own address on one envelope and put a £1 coin inside it (for protection). Fold, but do not seal the envelope, and place it inside the second envelope
- Write the following address on the second envelope, seal it carefully and post to:

I-Spy Books
Michelin Maps and Guides
Hannay House
39 Clarendon Road
Watford
WD17 1JA

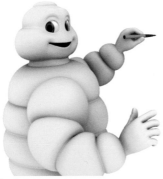